CW00665715

TRADES
and
PROFESSIONS
The Family Historians Guide

Stuart A. Raymond

THE FAMILY HISTORY PARTNERSHIP

Published by
The Family History Partnership LLP
P.O.Box 502
Bury, Lancashire
BL8 9EP

Webpage: **www.thefamilyhistorypartnership.co.uk**
Email: **sales@the familyhistorypartnership.com**

In association with
S.A. & M.J.Raymond
38 Princess Gardens
Hilperton, Trowbridge
Wiltshire BA14 7PT

Email: **samjraymond@btopenworld.com**

© S.A. & M.J. Raymond

ISBN: 978 1 906280 25 3

First published 2011

Printed and bound by Information Press
Southfield Road, Eynsham, Oxford OX29 4JB

Contents

Acknowledgements

My thanks to Richard Ratcliffe and Jane Starkey, who both read and commented on early drafts of this book. Thanks too to Bob Boyd, who has seen it through the press.

1. Introduction

Family history is more than just tracing family trees, and making sure that we know who is related to who. It also involves asking deeper questions. What did our ancestors do with their lives? What was their status in society? Did they have religious beliefs? Were they involved in official activities, such as being churchwardens or councillors? Did they migrate, and, if so, why? And what was their occupation? The latter question may be the most rewarding one to ask. Most of our ancestors worked for most of their lives. Work was a, perhaps the, major component of their lives. If you want to understand them, you need to understand the work that they did. You need to trace their training, their employment, their careers, how they passed their working days.

This book will help you do just that. There are innumerable sources which will help you trace occupational information about your ancestors. The aim here is to provide a broad description of what is available, where to find it, and how to use it.

The first step to discovering occupational information about your ancestors is to begin researching your family history. Read Stuart Raymond's *Introducing family history* (F.F.H.S., 2007) for a basic introductory guide. Ask your relatives and friends what they know. Check the records of civil registration and the census. The internet will help you with these, but make sure you use it critically. See 'The Internet: Reflections of an Old-timer' **www.familyhistorypartnership.co.uk/hints02.html** for a useful critique.

Birth, marriage, and death certificates, and census schedules, indicate the occupations of ancestors. Occupations are also frequently identified in other genealogical sources, such as parish registers, wills, and monumental inscriptions. If you can discover your ancestors' occupations from these sources, then you may well be able to trace more information in occupational sources.

Many old occupations are now obsolete. Leggers, shearmen, and scribblers (other than authors!) have disappeared. If you come across an occupational term you do not understand, consult a dictionary of occupations. These give brief definitions of particular terms, and explain what was involved. A number are available:

- CULLING, JOYCE. *Occupations: a preliminary list*. 2nd ed. F.F.H.S., 1999.
- TWINING, ANDREW, & TWINING, SANDRA. *Dictionary of old trades and occupations*. Twinings Secretarial, 1993.
- WATERS, C. *A dictionary of old trades, titles and occupations*. Rev. ed. Countryside Books, 2002.

Once you have identified your ancestors' occupations, you are in a position to search for occupational sources. Some are available on the internet, but it is likely that you will also have to visit libraries and record offices. A wide variety of sources are available. You may need to consult:

- personnel records
- the archives of trade guilds, professional associations, and trade unions
- governmental archives relating to the licensing and regulation of particular occupations
- books such as biographical dictionaries, trade directories, company histories, and parliamentary papers
- websites, especially those offering databases

Some sources, of course, are specific to particular occupations. Bishops' registers, for example, record the institutions of clergymen. Mines Inspectors reports list the names of miners who were victims of mining disasters. Professional yearbooks record the names of members of particular professions. In some instances, evidence comes initially from outside the library, for example, medals, trade tokens, makers marks on pottery, pipes, *etc.*

This book discusses some of the sources for particular occupations. It aims to demonstrate the wide diversity of sources available. It also lists the many genealogical guides - both books and websites - that provide more detailed help. It cannot, however, hope to be comprehensive. Most sources mentioned here can be found in libraries and/or record offices. An extensive collection of published sources is held by the Society of Genealogists. In the space of 61 pages, of course, it is not possible to mention every potential source. A much more comprehensive listing of published sources is provided by:

- RAYMOND, STUART A. *Occupational sources for genealogists: a bibliography.* 2nd ed. F.F.H.S., 1996.

Most volumes in this author's series of county bibliographies list works on occupations of local interest. Some of these volumes are solely devoted to occupational sources:

- RAYMOND, STUART A. *Londoners occupations: a genealogical guide.* 2nd ed. F.F.H.S., 2001,
- RAYMOND, STUART A. *Surrey and Sussex occupations: a genealogical guide.* F.F.H.S., 2001.
- RAYMOND, STUART A. *Yorkshire occupations: a genealogical guide.* F.F.H.S., 2000.

These bibliographies enable you to identify books that are likely to be relevant to your research. The books they list can usually be found in major reference libraries. Most library catalogues are available on the internet. For guidance in using libraries, consult:

- RAYMOND, STUART A. *Using libraries: workshops for family historians.* F.F.H.S., 2001.

Much information is available in public and university libraries, and in record offices. More specialist information is frequently held by companies, professional and trade organisations, and trade unions. Many of these organisations have their own libraries. Directories in which you can identify relevant libraries and archives include:

- FOSTER, JANET, & SHEPPARD, JULIA. *British archives: a guide to archives in the United Kingdom.* 4th ed. Palgrave, 2002.
- BLOOMFIELD, B.C., ed. *A directory of rare book and special collections in the United Kingdom and Republic of Ireland.* 2nd ed. Library Association Publishing, 1997.
- *ASLIB directory of information sources in the United Kingdom.* 14th ed. Routledge, 2006.

There is also a great deal of information available on the internet. Primary sources held by county record offices are listed at:

- A2A: access to archives
  www.nationalarchives.gov.uk/a2a

Many universities and colleges have extensive archival collections. These are listed at:

- Archives Hub
  www.archiveshub.ac.uk

For archives held in London, see:

- Aim 25: Archives in London and the M25 area
  www.aim25.ac.uk

Huge collections of archives relating to occupations can be found at :

- The National Archives
  www.nationalarchives.gov.uk

Other record office websites are listed at:

- English Record Offices and Archives on the Web
  www.oz.net/~markhow/englishros.htm

Detailed guidance on using the internet is provided by:

- RAYMOND, STUART A. *Netting your ancestors: tracing family history on the internet.* Family History Partnership, 2007.

Over 400 websites relating to occupations (most of them either guides to specific sources, or databases) are listed in:

- RAYMOND, STUART A. *Family history on the web: an internet directory for England & Wales.* 5th ed. Family History Partnership, 2008. There are companion volumes for Ireland and Scotland.

2. Life Cycle Occupations

A logical first step in discussing ancestral ocupations is to examine a number of what might be called 'life cycle occupations'. These are occupations which many, if not most, young men experienced in the past. The great majority of our nineteenth- and twentieth-century ancestors attended school. Many were apprenticed to a trade. Many also served in the armed forces, especially in war-time, before settling down into civilian life. It is therefore quite likely that the records of education, apprenticeship, and the armed services will all throw light on your family history.

2A. Scholars

The word is carefully chosen to head this section, as that is how schoolchildren were described in nineteenth-century census schedules. It is quite possible that someone in your family has educational memorabilia which has been passed down - books given as school prizes, examination certificates, school photographs, *etc*. These may help you to identify particular schools.

Schools left records. Those records, where they survive, are most likely to be found in record offices. Detailed listings of surviving records can be found by consulting the websites listed above, p. 7-8.

School records include admission and discharge registers, which are likely to provide details of ancestors' ages, addresses, and parents. Log books record the progress of schools from day to day, and sometimes include details of pupils' behaviour - or misbehaviour! There may also be other records - correspondence, punishment books, records of examinations, *etc*. London County Council School admission & discharge registers are amongst the sources indexed at

- London Generations
  **www.cityoflondon.gov.uk/Corporation/LGNL_Services/
  Leisure_and_culture/Records_and_archives/
  london_generations.htm**

A handful of registers for state schools have been published, for example:

- *East Stonehouse admission register 1866-1876*. Devon Family History Society, 2002.

There are published registers for many public schools. These sometimes include much biographical information. Similar registers are available for the alumni of Oxford and Cambridge, and for a number of other universities. Numerous public school and university registers are listed in:

- JACOBS, P.M. *Registers of the universities, colleges and schools of Great Britain and Ireland.* Athlone Press, 1964.

An extensive collection of school registers is held by the Society of Genealogists. These are listed in:
- *School, university, and college registers and histories in the library of the Society of Genealogists.* 1988.

For a full listing of the records of London's schools, see:
- WEBB, CLIFF. *An index of London schools and their records.* 3rd ed. Society of Genealogists Enterprises, 2007.

A similar list for the Diocese of Rochester is provided by:
- *School records: a supplement to West Kent sources; a guide to the location of school records in the Diocese of Rochester.* North West Kent Family History Society, 2004.

A number of websites offer information on university alumni. For students from Oxford, download a facsimile of the printed *Alumni Oxonienses* from:
- Alumni Oxonienses: The Members of the University of Oxford, 1500-1714: Their Parentage ... (1892)
  www.archive.org/
  Search 'Alumni Oxonienses'. Also includes 1715-1886

For the University of Cambridge, consult:
- Cambridge University Alumni, 1261-1900
  http://search.ancestry.co.uk/search/db.aspx?dbid=3997

Lists of University of London students are digitised at:
- University of London Student Records 1836-1926
  www.shl.lon.ac.uk/specialcollections/archives/ studentrecords.shtml

An overall view of educational records is provided by:
- CHAPMAN, COLIN. *The growth of British education and its records.* 2nd ed. Lochin Publishing, 1992.

See also:
- CHAPMAN, COLIN. *Using education records.* Basic facts about ... series. F.F.H.S., 1999.

2B. Apprentices

From the fourteenth century onwards, most tradesmen and craftsmen served an apprenticeship. Men who had not done so were not allowed to trade, and were fined if they did so. A boy entering an apprenticeship was bound to his master by an indenture, generally for seven years. His parents (or, if he was a pauper, his parish) may have had to pay a premium to bind the boy. A relitively small number of private indentures survive. However, registers of apprentices admitted to the freedom of city companies abound. Cliff Webb is currently indexing *London livery company apprenticeship registers*, and has so far completed over 50 volumes. These indexes have been published by the Society of Genealogists.

Most are also available online:
- London Apprenticeship Abstracts 1442-1850
  www.londonorigins.com/help/popup-aboutbo-lonapps.htm

London apprenticeship records are fully described on Guildhall Library's webpage:
- Sources for tracing apprenticeship and membership in city livery compa nies and related organisations
  www.history.ac.uk/gh/livdet.html

Apprenticeship indentures should have been enrolled. This was normally only done in towns and cities. Some registers have survived, and been published. See, for example:
- BARLOW, JILL. *A calendar of the registers of apprentices of the City of Gloucester.* Bristol and Gloucestershire Record Society, **14**. 2001.

- RISING, WINIFRED M., & MILLICAN, PERCY, eds. *An index of indentures of Norwich apprentices enrolled with the Norwich Assembly, Henry VII-George II.* Norfolk Record Society, **29**. 1959.

A collection of apprenticeship indentures for Westminster held by the Society of Genealogists is described in:
- CHURCHILL, ELSE. '*Munimenta antiqua* and Crisp's collections of original apprenticeship indentures 1641-1999, and original marriage licences', *Genealogists' magazine* **28**(3), 2004, p.101-3.

Young people could also be apprenticed by the poor law authorities. Apprenticeship provided the overseers with a means of looking after orphans and other young paupers. Apprenticeship indentures survive amongst the records of parishes and poor law unions. So do the registers which parish overseers were directed to keep by an act of 1801-2. These continue to 1844, when compulsory apprenticeship was abolished. They contain similar information to indentures, but - crucially - include the names of parents, which were excluded from indentures. A number of these registers have been published, especially by Devon Family History Society; see, for example:

- *Ashton apprentices register 1804-1841*. Devon Family History Society, 2005.

Businesses and charities may also hold records of apprentices. The records of a Wiltshire charity which apprenticed the children of deserving parents to masters in Wiltshire and London are calendared in:

- HENLY, H.R., ed. *The apprentice registers of the Wiltshire Society, 1817-1922*. Wiltshire Record Society **51**. 1997.

Between 1710 and 1811, stamp duty was imposed on apprenticeship indentures. Registers of the duties paid were kept. These are now in the National Archives (TNA), and are fully described in:

- Apprenticeship Records as Sources for Genealogy
  www.nationalarchives.gov.uk/catalogue/researchguidesindex.asp
  (click title)

Abstracts from these registers to 1774 are now available online at:

- British Origins
  www.britishorigins.com

A few record societies have published extracts from these registers. See, for example:

- DALE, CHRISTABEL, ed. *Wiltshire apprentices and their masters 1710-1760*. Wiltshire Archaeological and Natural History Society Records Branch **17**. 1961.

Up until c.1745-1750, the name, occupation and place of origin of the father (designated "deceased" where appropriate), guardian or widowed mother of the apprentice is usually given. The name, occupation and place of work of the master is given throughout the series. More than 1,000,000 names are listed in the original registers. For a full discussion of apprenticeship records, see:

- RAYMOND, STUART A. *My ancestor was an apprentice*. Society of Genealogists, forthcoming

See also:
- GIBBENS, LILIAN. 'Records of apprenticeship: a lesser-used source', *Family history news & digest* **10**(4), 1996, p.167-71.
- GOLLAND, JIM. 'Compell'd to weep ...': the apprenticeship system', *Genealogists' magazine* **23**(4), 1989, p.121-7.

2C. The Army

Until the mid-twentieth century, Englishmen had always been under an obligation to bear arms in defence of the realm. Consequently, most of us have ancestors who fought in the wars - and especially in the First World War. Surviving records of the army are extensive, and are a vital source of information for all family historians. No attempt will be made to describe them here. It will be much better to use the limited space available to identify the books and websites most likely to help with research.

There are many published guides and handbooks. Amongst the most generally useful are:
- FOWLER, SIMON. *Tracing your army ancestors*. Pen & Sword, 2006.
- PATERSON, SARAH. *Tracing your family history: Army*. Imperial War Museum, 2006.
- SPENCER, WILLIAM. *Army records: a guide for family historians*. The National Archives, 2008.
- WATTS, MICHAEL, & WATTS, CHRISTOPHER J. *My ancestor was in the British Army: how can I find out more about him?* 2nd ed. Society of Genealogists Enterprises, 2009.

For a database of medieval soldiers, consult:
- The Soldier in Later Medieval England
  www.icmacentre.ac.uk/soldier/database

Nineteenth century records are described in:
- GOLDSMITH, JEREMY. 'The Commander-in-Chief's memoranda at The National Archives', *Genealogists' magazine* **29**(4), 2007, 141-5.

For First World War records, see:
- SPENCER, WILLIAM. *Army service records of the First World War*. 3rd ed. The National Archives, 2001.
- HOLDING, NORMAN. *World War I army ancestry*. 4th ed. F.F.H.S., 2003.
- HOLDING, NORMAN. *More sources of World War I army ancestry*. 3rd ed. FFHS, 1998.

Records not in TNA are listed in:
- HOLDING, NORMAN H. *The location of British Army Records 1914-1918.* 4th ed. FFHS, 1999.

For the Second World War, consult:
- FOWLER, SIMON. *Tracing your Second World War ancestors.* Countryside Books, 2006.

Sources for ancestors who fought in other wars are described in:
- TOMASELLI, PHIL. *The Crimean War, 1854-56.* Military history sources for family historians. F.F.H.S., 2006.

- TOMASELLI, PHIL. *The Zulu War, 1879.* Military history sources for family historians. F.F.H.S., 2006.

- TOMASELLI, PHIL. *The Anglo-Boer War, 1899-1902.* Military history sources for family historians. F.F.H.S., 2006.

Most military records are held at TNA. Many useful 'research signposts' on military history are listed at:
- National Archives: Looking for a Person
  www.nationalarchives.gov.uk/records/looking-for-person

These include:
- British Army officers up to 1913
- British Army officers after 1913
- British Army soldiers up to 1913
- British Army soldiers after 1913
- British Army nurses
- Women in the British Army
- Women's Land Army
- Home Guard Militia
- Indian army
- African forces under British control

There are also a number of in depth research guides at:
www.nationalarchives.gov.uk/catalogue/researchguidesindex.asp.
These include, amongst others:
- British Army: Officers' Records 1660-1913
- British Army: Officers' Commissions
- British Army Lists

A number of sources for soldiers have been digitised for web pages. TNA's own 'Documents Online' site **www.nationalarchives.gov.uk/documentsonline** has digitised images of:
- World War I Campaign Medals
- Selected First World War and Army of Occupation War Diaries
- World War I Prisoner of War interviews
- Recommendations for Honours and Awards, 1935-1980
- World War I Women's (later Queen Mary's) Army Auxiliary Corps
- Royal Hospital Chelsea: Selected Soldiers' Service Records

'Ancestry' **www.ancestry.co.uk** has many databases of digitised military sources. The most important of these are:
- British Army World War One Service Records, 1914-1920
- British Army World War One Medal Rolls Index Cards, 1914-1920
- British Army World War One Pension Records 1914-1920
- Soldiers Died in the Great War, 1914-1919

'Find My Past' **www.findmypast.com** also has a number of important data-bases:
- Soldiers Died in the Great War 1914-1918 (also on 'Ancestry')
- National Roll of the Great War 1914-1918
- Armed Forces Births Marriages & Deaths
- Waterloo Medal Roll 1815

The Commonwealth War Graves Commission 'Debt of Honour register' **www.cwgc.org** has the details of 1,700,000 service people who died during the two world wars, and of the 23,000 cemeteries, memorials and other locations worldwide where they are commemorated. It can also be searched for details of 67,000 civilians who died as a result of enemy action in the Second World War.

There are a number of other important war memorial sites. These include:
- The British War Memorial Project
  http://warmemorial.wordpress.com/2007/02/23/british-war-memorial-project
- Roll of Honour
  www.roll-of-honour.com
- UK National Inventory of War Memorials
  www.ukniwm.org.uk

There are numerous other web pages devoted to military history. They are listed in:
- FOWLER, SIMON. *A guide to military history on the internet.* Pen & Sword, 2007.

3. Personnel and Business Records

Employers keep records of their employees. Many personnel records have been deposited in record offices. Surviving records are extensive, although of course many more have been lost. Increasing government regulation in the late nineteenth and early twentieth centuries encouraged the more systematic keeping of records. Even before this, some records do survive. Employers' records include a variety of documents:

- wages book
- registers of employees (including separate registers of apprentices *etc*)
- applications for jobs
- service and pension records
- rolls of honour
- annual reports and company magazines

Company records supply us with the names, not just of employees, but also of directors, shareholders, and customers. There are several useful introductions to these records. One is written specifically for family historians:

- PROBERT, E.D. *Company and business records for family historians.* F.F.H.S., 1994.

See also:

- ARMSTRONG, J., & JONES, S. *Business documents.* Mansell, 1987.
- ORBELL, JOHN. *A guide to tracing the history of a business.* Gower, 1987.

Information about companies, giving names of directors and shareholders, has been collected under various companies acts. Historic records relating to company registration are described in TNA's leaflet:

- Registration of Companies and Businesses
  www.nationalarchives.gov.uk/catalogue/researchguidesindex.asp
  (click title)

For a general introduction to the records of the Registrar of Companies, see:

- WATTS, CHRISTOPHER, & WATTS, MICHAEL J. 'Company records as a source of family history', *Genealogists' magazine* **21**(2), 1983, p.44-54.

Many surviving collections of business archives are listed in:

- RICHMOND, LESLEY, & STOCKFORD, BRIDGET. *Company archives: the survey of the records of 1000 of the first registered companies in England and Wales.* Gower, 1986.

The Business Archives Council **www.businessarchivescouncil.org.uk/ publications/complete** has sponsored a number of guides to the records of particular occupations. These include:

- HABGOOD, WENDY. *Chartered accountants in England and Wales: a guide to historical records.* Manchester University Press, 1994.
- RICHMOND. LESLEY, & TURTON, ALISON. *The brewing industry: a guide to historical records.* Manchester University Press, 1990.
- RICHMOND, LESLEY, STEVENSON, JULIE, & TURTON, ALISON. *The Pharmaceutical industry. A guide to historical records.* Ashgate, 2003.
- HUNTER, PAMELA. *Veterinary medicine: a guide to the historical records.* Ashgate, 2004.

Some employers maintain their own archives, and devote considerable resources to them. Examples include:

- British Postal Museum and Archive
  www.postalheritage.org.uk
- Devon and Cornwall Constabulary Heritage & Learning Resource
  www.policeheritagecentre.co.uk
- National Gas Archive
  www.gasarchive.org

Local record offices hold the personnel records of many local firms, and also those of local councils. Record office web pages sometimes give details. See, for example:

- Cheshire West & Chester: Railways Staff Register
  www.cheshirewestandchester.gov.uk/council_services/record_ office/catalogues_and_indexes/railways_staff_database.aspx

- Durham County Record Office: Colliery Personnel Records
  www.durham-pa.gov.uk/recordoffice/usp.nsf/pws/ Durham+Record+Office+-+Our+Holdings+-+Information+ Leaflets+-+PDF+Format
  (click 'title')

For the public sector, TNA holds civil service and armed forces records, as well as the archives of many nationalised companies. There are research guides on its website for the personnel records of civil servants, coastguards, customs & excise officials and tax collectors, the Metropolitan Police, transport police, railwaymen, Royal Naval Dockyards, and royal warrant holders & household servants. Visit:

- The National Archives: Research Guides A-Z
  www.nationalarchives.gov.uk/catalogue/researchguidesindex.asp

Many histories of particular companies have been written. These provide the background against which the careers of their employees must be understood. They often include details of personnel, and are listed in:

- GOODALL, FRANCIS. *A bibliography of British business histories.* Aldershot: Gower, 1987.
- ZARACH, STEPHANIE. *Debrett's bibliography of British business history.* Macmillan, 1986.

4. Government Regulation

Over the centuries, governments have sought to regulate a variety of occupations. Their motives have been various. Seamen have been registered so that they could be recruited for the Royal Navy in time of need. Entry to the medical professions has been tightly controlled to ensure that practitioners are competent. Clergy, teachers, and others have been checked for soundness of doctrine and their loyalty to the crown. The names of directors of limited companies are registered by the Companies Registrar to ensure their probity. Licences have been required by innkeepers, printers, and badgers (i.e.pedlars), amongst others. The bureaucrats have left behind extensive archives, which provide much information on the occupations that have been regulated.

Bishops, Quarter Sessions, and local councils have all issued licences to engage in particular occupations. Diocesan archives are likely to include records of licences issued by bishops to curates, surgeons, midwives, and teachers. Quarter Sessions had reponsibility for licencing printers, badgers, innkeepers, gamekeepers, drovers, game dealers, and lunatic asylums. More recently, local councils have acquired powers to licence a wide range of activities, such as grocers and taxi drivers, tram drivers and conductors, poisons and pharmacists. Registers of licences will provide details such as addresses and dates, and may enable you to trace the careers of particular ancestors. They are mostly held in local record offices.

Regulation at the national level has affected a number of occupations. TNA's website **www.nationalarchives.gov.uk/catalogue/researchguidesindex. asp** has 'research guides' relating to a number of regulated occupations:
- Education: records of teachers
- Lawyers: records of attorneys and solicitors
- Lunatic Asylums, 18th-20th centuries
- National Farm Surveys of England and Wales, 1940-1943
- Merchant Seamen: records of the Registry of Shipping and Seamen

Information relating to occupations can also be found in TNA's guides on
- Bankruptcy Records after 1869
- Bankrupts and Insolvent Debtors 1710-1869
- Registration of Companies and Businesses

Acts of Parliament sometimes required the publication of lists of registered professions. The *Medical register* has been published regularly since 1859, the *Den-*

tists register since 1879, and the *Register of nurses* since 1922. Digitised images of the *Medical register* for 1913, and the *Dentists register* for 1925, are available at:

- Find My Past
  **www.findmypast.com/helpadvice/knowledge-base/
  adoptions-directories/index.jsp#occupations**
  (scroll down)

The Education Act 1899 made provision for the registration of teachers. The Teachers Registration Council operated from then until 1948 (with a gap 1907-12), and recorded details of 100,000 teachers. Some of these had been teachers since the 1870s. The names registered can be searched at:

- British Origins: Teachers Registrations
  www.originsnetwork.com/help/aboutbo-teachers.aspx

5. Trade Guilds, Professional Associations, and Trade Unions

People who are engaged in the same occupation frequently form associations in order to promote their interests. Independent tradesmen, such as butchers and bakers, form guilds. Professional associations are formed by those whose occupations require extensive formal education, such as accountants and engineers. Trade unions are formed by workers and tradesmen who are employed by other people. All of these organizations have recorded the names of their members, and left archives detailing their activities.

Craft guilds originated in the thirteenth and fourteenth centuries. They should not be confused with religious guilds, although sometimes they did organize religious services, and had their own priests. They were essentially associations of tradesmen established to regulate a particular trade. They usually controlled admission to the trade in question through the apprenticeship system, discussed above. Frequently they had monopoly powers over the trade in their particular town or city, and could prevent non-members from trading. They provided for their members in sickness or old age, and for their members' children. Sometimes they ran their own schools. The members of a city's guilds were frequently automatically freemen of the city. They can therefore be traced in registers of freemen. Some of these have been published, e.g.

- ROWE, MARGERY M., & JACKSON, ANDREW M., eds. *Exeter freemen, 1266-1967.* Devon & Cornwall Record Society, extra series, **1**. 1973.

For London, reference may be made to:
- ALDOUS, VIVIENNE E. *My ancestors were freemen of the City of London: how can I find out more about them?* Society of Genealogists, 1999.

London's guilds were particularly numerous. Many are still active, but modern members rarely follow the relevant trade. Most lost their trade connections in the late eighteenth or nineteenth centuries. A basic historical introduction to the guilds of London is provided by:
- MELLING, J.K. *Discovering London's guilds and liveries.* 6th ed. Shire, 2003.

Much has been written on the guilds of London. A detailed bibliography, with a useful historical introduction, is provided by:
- KAHL, WILLIAM F. *The development of London livery companies: an historical essay and a select bibliography.* Kress Library of Business and Economics publication **15**. Baker Library, Harvard Graduate School of Business Administration, 1960.

Guilds created records. Apprenticeship records have already been discussed; these, and admittances to the freedom of the company, are the most useful records for genealogical purposes. Other records include alphabetical lists of freemen, quarterage books (listing members for a particular year), and court minute books. For information on guild records in London, visit:

- Livery Company Membership Guide
  www.history.ac.uk/gh/livintro.htm

A more detailed guide is provided by
- *City livery companies and related organisations: a guide to their archives in Guildhall Library.* 3rd ed. Guildhall Library, 1989.

Livery Company members are listed in the City's annual poll books, which record the names of voters, and run from the late seventeenth century until 1872, and which are held by Guildhall Library. The liverymen were also entitled to vote in Parliamentary elections. These were less frequent, but are also recorded in poll-books. One Parliamentary poll book for London is currently available in facsimile:
- *The London poll book 1768.* S.A. & M.J.Raymond, [1996].

Many others are listed in:
- GIBSON, JEREMY, & ROGERS, COLIN. *Poll books 1696-1872: a directory of holdings in Great Britain.* 4th ed. Family History Partnership, 2008.

Numerous professional associations were formed in the nineteenth and twentieth centuries. Their role frequently included examining and admitting new entrants to the profession. Many issued yearbooks which listed their members. Their journals frequently contained obituaries of members. Sometimes separate lists of members were issued. Administrative records such as committee minutes and subscription books may contain information about people. Organisations such as the Institution of Mechanical Engineers **www.imeche.org**, the British Dental Association **www.bda.org**, and the Royal Institute of British Architects **www.architecture.com** have libraries and record offices where historical records relating to the admittance of members can be examined.

Trade unions also date from the nineteenth century. Their role involved not only protecting their members rights at work, but also insuring them against sickness and death. Their records include minutes recording the admission of new members, registers of contributions received, journals and annual reports which may contain obituaries, lists of members receiving benefits, *etc*. There are a number of published histories of trade unions, which are worth consulting if your ancestor was a member.

The archives of many trade unions have been deposited in the Modern Records

Centre of the University of Warwick. These include, for example, the Operative Bricklayers Society, the Amalgamated Society of Lithographic Printers, and the National Association of Operative Plasterers. See:

- Family History at the Modern Records Centre
  www2.warwick.ac.uk/services/library/mrc/subject_guides/ family_history

The records of a number of unions are deposited with London Metropolitan University. These are listed at **www.aim25.ac.uk**. A detailed listing of trade union records deposited in libraries and record offices (albeit a little out of date) is provided by:

- SOUTHALL, HUMPHREY, GILBERT, DAVID, & BRYCE, CAROL. *Nineteenth century trade union records: an introduction and select guide.* Historical geography research series **27**. Historical Geography Research Group, 1994.

If you want to know more about trade union ancestors, visit:

- Trade Union Ancestors
  www.unionancestors.co.uk

A more detailed discusssion is provided by:

- CRAIL, MARK. *Tracing your Labour Movement ancestors: a guide for family historians.* Pen & Sword, 2009.

6. Books & Journals

There is an extraordinarily wide range of books on specific occupations. Many offer general histories and/or descriptive accounts. Shire Books have published many titles in this category, such as Kenneth Kilby's *Coopers and coopering* (2004) or Richard Williams' *Lime kilns and lime burning* (2nd ed. 2004). Harry Hanson's *Canal boatmen 1760-1914* (Manchester University Press, 1975) is another example of the genre, as is Alison Grant's *North Devon pottery: the seventeenth century* (University of Exeter, 1983). Such books help us to understand how our ancestors lived. A useful, if rather out of date, bibliography of such books is provided by

- JEWELL, ANDREW. *Crafts, trades, and industries: a book list for local historians*. National Council of Social Service, 1968.

Direct information about a variety of old trades and professions is provided by:
- HURLEY, BERYL, ed. *The book of trades, or library of useful arts, 1811.* 3 vols. Wiltshire Family History Society, 1991-4.

General books on particular occupations frequently do not provide information of direct genealogical value. They are useful as general background, but not for the specifics of tracing particular individuals. There are, however, innumerable books which are of direct use to genealogists. These include a rapidly increasing number of titles providing guidance on tracing ancestors in specific occupations. The volumes in the Society of Genealogists' *My ancestors ...* series are particularly useful. Numerous titles likely to be of use to family historians are listed in the bibliographies already mentioned (p.6).

Genealogical journals also frequently carry relevant articles. *Ancestors* was TNA's magazine. The *Genealogists' magazine* is published by the Society of Genealogists. *Family tree magazine* is the oldest of the commercial journals. Others include *Family history monthly, Your Family tree, Practical family history,* and *Who do you think you are? magazine.* All of these regularly publish articles on tracing people who worked in specific occupations. *Family history news and digest,* the journal of the Federation of Family History Societies, has unfortunately ceased publication. However, it frequently published authoritative articles on particular occupations (some of which are mentioned below). Its 'digest' section indexed the journals of the Federation's many member societies, which frequently have relevant articles. Back runs of all these journals can be found in many libraries.

7. Trade & Professional Journals

There are numerous trade and professional journals, for example, the *Drapers' record*, the *Library Association record*, and the *Brewers almanac*. These frequently include obituaries and death notices, advertisements, biographical notices, lists of the officers and/or members of trade organizations, and much background information on the particular occupations concerned. A similar function for churchmen is provided by denominational magazines, such as the *Methodist magazine* (1798-1821).

Most large libraries have runs of trade journals, but the most comprehensive collection is held by:

- British Library Newspaper Collection
  www.bl.uk/reshelp/findhelprestype/news/blnewscoll

8. Biographical Dictionaries

Biographical dictionaries generally include brief biographies of the individuals listed, usually giving information on birth, marriage and death dates, spouses and children. Many relate to specific occupations, for example:

- COLLISON, ROBERT L. *Who's who in librarianship.* Bowes & Bowes, [1954].
- COLVIN, H.M. *A biographical dictionary of British architects, 1600-1840.* Rev.ed. John Murray, 1978.
- GUNNIS, RUPERT. *Dictionary of British sculptors, 1660-1851.* New rev ed. Murrays, 1968.

A full listing is provided in:

- SLOCUM, ROBERT B. *Biographical dictionaries and related works.* Michigan, 1967. See also supplements, 1972 and 1978.

Numerous biographical dictionaries are indexed in:

- *Biography and genealogy master index: a consolidated index to more than 3,200,000 biographical sketches in over 350 current and retrospective biographical dictionaries.* 8 vols. Gale biographical index series **1**. 2nd ed. Gale Research, 1986.

9. Trade Directories

Trade directories were intended to put tradesmen in touch with their customers, and customers in touch with tradesmen. They generally list the names of the substantial householders of each of the towns and parishes they cover, with their occupations. The names of servants, labourers, and women, are not usually given.

Directories were published by a wide variety of different publishers. Kelly's is the best known, and published directories for most counties. There were also many local publishers who published directories for their own areas. Some were issued at regular intervals. Where that is the case, it should be possible to follow the career of tradesmen through successive issues of local directories.

A handful of historic directories have been reprinted. Many more have been reissued on CD by firms such as:
- S & N Genealogy Supplies
  www.genealogysupplies.com

Many directories on CD are listed in:
- RAYMOND, STUART A. *British family history on CD*. FFHS, 2001.

Many hundred directories have been digitised for the internet, and are fully searchable, at:
- Historical Directories
  www.historicaldirectories.org

Most local studies libraries and record offices have runs of directories for their own areas. They are listed in:
- NORTON, J.E. *Guide to the national and provincial directories of England and Wales, excluding London, before 1856*. Royal Historical guides and handbooks **5**. 1950.
- SHAW, G., & TIPPER, A. *British directories: a bibliography and guide to directories published in Ireland and Wales (1850-1950), and Scotland (1773-1950)*. Leicester University Press, 1988.

For London, see:
- ATKINS, P.J. *The directories of London, 1677-1855*. Mansell, 1990.

In addition to trade directories covering particular counties or cities, there were also directories devoted to particular occupations. Some examples are:
- *The Electrician electrical trades directory and handbook*. 1890-1926.

- *The Furnishing trade encyclopedia, who's who, diary and buyers guide.* 1936-1965.
- *Marchant & Co's metropolitan and provincial engineers, iron & metal trades directory.* Marchant, Singer & Co., 1857.

The work by Shaw & Tipper listed above has a valuable introduction to trade directories. For a more detailed review of their value and uses, see:

- SHAW, GARETH. *Directing the past: directories and the local historian.* British Association for Local History, 2003.

10. Parliamentary Papers

The *Parliamentary papers* constitute the largest ongoing project in British publishing. Thousands of papers are included in this series, from the late eighteenth century onwards. They include numerous reports from select committees and royal commissions. There are annual reports from government agencies, and white papers proposing new policies. Many papers are concerned with particular occupations. There are, for example, numerous reports relating to agriculture, to mining, and to children's employment. Evidence given to government commissions by our ancestors, and printed in the *Parliamentary papers*, may provide invaluable information for family historians. Ancestors may be identified in lists of staff printed in annual reports, or in the various other lists of names which found their way into these papers, e.g. the return of *Owners of land* made in 1872/3 (see below, p.44).

Runs of the *Parliamentary papers* are found in most large public reference and university libraries. Digitised images can be consulted online through:

- House of Commons Parliamentary Papers
  http://parlipapers.chadwyck.co.uk/marketing/index.jsp

This is a commercial database, charging substantial fees, but you may be able to get free access through your local public library. For a detailed listing of Parliamentary papers, see:

- Bopcris Digitisation Projects: Ford selections of British Parliamentary Papers
  www.southampton.ac.uk/library/bopcris/projects.html
  (click 'Bopcris Ford Collection')

For the ninetenth century, see also:

- COCKTON, PETER. *Subject catalogue of the House of Commons Parliamentary papers 1800-1900.* 5 vols. Chadwyck-Healy, 1988.

11. Indexes

Many indexes to sources for specific occupations, such as blacksmiths and gun-makers, have been compiled. Indexes may be in print, on the internet, or unpublished. Several pages are devoted to listing them in:

- GIBSON, JEREMY. *Specialist indexes for family historians.* 3rd ed. Family History Partnership, forthcoming.

12. Sources for Specific Occupations

Many occupations have sources which are unique to them, although most would fall into the categories discussed above. An extraordinarily wide range of sources are available. The list which follows is indicative of what you might be able to find; it is far from being comprehensive, and cannot hope to mention every source. It does, however, attempt to indicate where you can find further information. Much more information may be tracked down by using the bibliographies listed above (p.6), and the many other books and websites cited here.

Accountants
The Institute of Chartered Accountants has collected 3,200 obituaries of accountants for the period 1875-1965 for a web-based database. See:
- Accountancy Ancestors
  www.icaew.com/index.cfm/route/155615/icaew_ga/en/Home/ About_us/History_of_accounting/Accountancy_Ancestors

Agricultural Labourers
Labourers working in agriculture are frequently referred to as 'ag labs', as this was the abbreviation used by census enumerators in the nineteenth century. It has been widely assumed that researching agricultural labourers is difficult. It is true that there are few sources which are specific to this occupation. However, there are many sources which can be used to trace them. A detailed guide is provided by:
- WALLER, IAN H. *My ancestor was an agricultural labourer*. Society of Genealogists Enterprises, 2007.

For a briefer summary, see:
- Best Websites for Agricultural Labourers
  www.bbcwhodoyouthinkyouaremagazine.com/take-it-further/ jobs/best-websites-agricultural-labourers

Airmen
For RAF ancestors, most records are in TNA. They include service records and unit records. Two useful research guides are available on TNA's site
  www.nationalarchives.gov.uk/catalogue/researchguidesindex.asp
  These are:
- Royal Air Force, RFC and RNAS Service Records: First World War, 1914-1918
- Royal Air Force Service Records: Second World War, 1939-1945

A number of important sources have been digitised for TNA's 'Documents Online' database **www.nationalarchives.gov.uk/documentsonline**. These include, amongst others, the World War I service records of some 99,000 Royal Air Force officers, and 30,000 service records of the Womens Royal Air Force 1918-1920.

A few records, including First World War casualty cards, and personal papers, are held by:

- Royal Air Force Museum
  www.rafmuseum.org.uk

A roll of honour for airmen of World War I is printed in:

- HOBSON, CHRIS. *Airmen died in the Great War 1914-1918: the roll of honour of the British and Commonwealth Air Services of the First World War*. J.B.Hayward & Son, 1995.

Officers are regularly listed in:

- *The monthly Air Force list*. 1919-30. Continued as *Air Force list*. 1931-

There are a number of published guides to RAF records:

- SPENCER, WILLIAM. *Air Force Records for Family Historians*. Public Record Office, 2000.
- TOMASELLI, PHIL. *Tracing your Air Force ancestors*. Pen & Sword, 2007.
- WOOTTON, ANGELA. *Tracing your family history: Royal Air Force*, ed. Sarah Paterson. Imperial War Museum, 2006.

Architects

An architect's archives can form a major source for biographical information. Letters, diaries, and other papers can provide invaluable information. The Royal Institute of British Architects holds many collections of architects' papers, as well as the election papers of RIBA members. The latter frequently include information on the professional education, practice, architectural and literary works of particular architects. For details of the RIBA archives, see:

- RIBA Archives: Biographical
  www.architecture.com/LibraryDrawingsAndPhotographs/ DrawingsAndArchives/Archives/Biographical.aspx

Artists

There are many archival collections of papers created by artists, Such papers include correspondence, personal and professional notes, diaries, sketchbooks, ledgers, bills, annotations in books and journals, press cuttings, and photographs. These collections are listed at:

- Artists Papers Database
  www.aah.org.uk/page/2765

Authors

Authors are exceptionally well documented. Family historians should be continually using one of the major sources of information about them - library catalogues. Catalogues not only list the books that authors wrote, but also frequently give birth and/or death dates, or at least indicate when an author was actively writing. They may also give alternative names, and sometimes other occupations. These are the methods that librarians use in order to distinguish different authors with the same names. The best catalogues to consult to check this type of information are those of major research institutions, such as the British Library **catalogue.bl.uk** and the Library of Congress **catalog.loc.gov**.

Bankers

Bankers can be traced through bank archives. These include staff registers, which may give a great deal of information - perhaps even photographs. They also include salary lists, apprenticeship indentures, declarations of secrecy, fidelity bonds, and many other documents. For a brief overview of banking records, consult:
- Banking Ancestors
  www.bbcwhodoyouthinkyouaremagazine. com/take-it-further/jobs/banking-ancestors

Banks generally still hold their archives (which also, incidentally, include much information about their customers). These are private, but banks may allow you to consult them. Many collections are listed in:
- PRESSNELL, L.S., & ORBELL, JOHN. *A guide to the historical records of British banking.* Gower, 1985.

A number of banks give details of their archives on their webpages. See, for example:
- Bank of England Archives
  www.bankofengland.co.uk/about/history/archive
- Royal Bank of Scotland: Our Archives
  www.rbs.com/about-rbs/g2/heritage.ashx
  (click 'Our Archives')

The minute books of the Ionian Bank's Court of Directories, 1839-1917, have been digitised for the internet. These record, amongst much else, the appointments of directors and managers. See:
- Ionian Bank Court of Directors minute books
  www.lse.ac.uk/library/archive/online_resources/IBminutebks. aspx

Bevin Boys
Not everyone who was conscripted during the Second World War served in the armed forces. About 48,000 went down the mines. An attempt to trace them is being made by:
- Bevin Boys Association
  www.seniorsnetwork.co.uk/bevinboys

Some records about them are held in TNA. See:
- Bevin Boys
  http://yourarchives.nationalarchives.gov.uk/index.php?title= Bevin_Boys

For more information, consult:
- GARNER, KATH. 'At the coal face', *Family history monthly* **135**, 2006, p.22-5.

Blacksmiths
The genealogical endeavours of Ann Spiro have produced a large database listing blacksmiths, cartwrights, wheelwrights, shipwrights, farriers, iron workers, and related tradesmen. This database is based primarily on census returns, and can be found at:
- The Blacksmiths Index
  http://freepages.genealogy.rootsweb.ancestry.com/~blacksmiths

Boatmen
See also Watermen
Various eighteenth and nineteenth century acts required the registration of narrow boats with local authorities. Most of the registers created are in local record offices, and give owner's names.

A major collection of archives relating to waterways is held by:
- The National Waterways Musem
  www.nwm.org.uk

Archives relating to waterways from 14 different record offices are catalogued at:
- Virtual Waterways Archive Catalogue
  www.virtualwaterways.co.uk

A guide to researching canal boatmen can be found on the website of the London Canal Museum:
- Family History: a checklist for researchers
  www.canalmuseum.org.uk/collection/family-history.htm

It is also worth consulting:
- TRINDER, BARRIE. 'Boatpeople: from the 17th to the 19th century', *Genealogists' magazine* **23**(10), 1991, p.374-5.

Book Trades
Numerous publications devoted to the book trades prior to 1851 have been indexed in order to compile:
- British Book Trade Index
  www.bbti.bham.ac.uk

Book trade apprentices whose names appear in the Inland Revenue apprenticeship registers (see above, p.xxx) are listed in:
- MAXTED, IAN. *The British book trades, 1710-1777*. The author, 1983.

Brewers, Publicans & Victuallers
A basic introduction to researching ancestors in breweries and pubs is provided by:
- FOWLER, SIMON. *Researching brewery and publican ancestors*. 2nd ed. Family History Partnership, 2009.

Licencing records are found with the records of Quarter Sessions and County Councils, in county record offices. They will enable you to trace the career of an innkeeper. A guide to locations is provided by:
- GIBSON, JEREMY, & HUNTER, JUDITH. *Victuallers licences: records for family and local historians*. 3rd ed. Family History Partnership, 2009.

For a local guide to sources, which has information potentially useful to researchers nation-wide, see Buckinghamshire Record Office's website:
- Public Houses in Buckinghamshire: a Short Guide to Sources
  www.buckscc.gov.uk/bcc/archives/Public_Houses.page

For London, see:
- Licensed Victuallers Records
  www.cityoflondon.gov.uk/Corporation/LGNL_Services/ Leisure_and_culture/Records_and_archives/Visitor_ information/free_information_leaflets.htm
  (click title)

Brokers
Brokers were men who dealt in particular commodities, such as tea, sugar or stocks. Their activities in the City of London were regulated by the Corporation of

London. Records survive from medieval times. Between 1697 and 1886, acts of Parliament required brokers to be licenced by the Court of Aldermen. The London Metropolitan Archives hold six volumes of admission registers, 1708-1869, with names, addresses, dates of admission, and details of sureties. There is also an index to some 8000 names in brokers' bonds, and a set of ledgers of brokers' rents. The latter record the annual 'rent' brokers had to pay, and sometimes note dates of death. See:

- Sworn Brokers Archives
  www.cityoflondon.gov.uk/Corporation/LGNL_Services/ Leisure_and_culture/Records_and_archives/Visitor_ information/free_information_leaflets.htm
  (click title)

Brushmakers

The Society of Brushmakers Descendants **www.brushmakers.com** is dedicated to tracing brushmakers, and has a couple of useful pages on its website. Brushmakers can be traced through trade union records, some of which are held by:

- The Working Class Movement Library
  www.wcml.org.uk/holdings/brushmakers

Builders

The *Builder* was a periodical first published in 1843, which regularly reported on new buildings. It was particularly noted for its illustrations, and was read by many outside the industry who were interested in modern architecture. Many people are mentioned: architects, sculptors, heating engineers, carpenters, *etc.* The journal has been fully indexed. If your ancestor was a builder, or involved in the construction industry, it may be worthwhile to check:

- RICHARDSON, RUTH, & THORNE, ROBERT. *The Builder illustrations index, 1843-1883*. The Builder Group / Hutton & Rostron, 1994.

Butchers

The *Meat trades journal*, which has been regularly published since 1888, is the principal journal for butchers. It contains obituaries, notes on wills, biographies of prominent butchers, details of bankruptcies, and notes on the dissolution of partnerships.

Butchers may also be traced in Quarter Sessions records. Slaughter houses required a licence from a JP after 1786. Slaughterhouse keepers had to keep an account of every animal slaughtered. Ministers and churchwardens might be called upon to certify an applicant's fitness to hold a licence. Register books, certificates from ministers and churchwardens, and slaughter house keepers books survive, as do the records of inspectors. There are a variety of other records which may help

you to trace a butcher. Trade directories should enable you to trace a butcher's career in the nineteenth and early twentieth centuries. Newspapers may also provide clues. These and other sources are discussed in:
- GIBBONS, SUE. 'Butchers', *Family history monthly* **78**, 2002, p.6-11.

Circus Workers
See also Theatrical Workers
Research on circus workers relies on a number of large collections of ephemera such as posters, handbills, and programmes. Details of these collections can be found on their websites:
- Victoria & Albert Museum: Collections: Theatre and Performance
  www.vam.ac.uk/collections/theatre_performance/
- National Fairground Archive
  www.nfa.dept.shef.ac.uk

There are a large number of books on the circus, held in many libraries. These are listed in:
- TOOLE STOTT, R. *Circus and allied arts: a world bibliography [1500-1970].* 5 vols. Vol. 1-4 published Harpur & Sons (Derby) Ltd., 1958-1971; Vol. 5 published Circus Friends Association of Great Britain, 1992.

Sources are discussed in detail by:
- TURNER, JOHN. 'Circuses, circus families, and the circus showmen', *Family history news & digest* **14**(3), 2004, p.102-5.

It may also be useful to visit:
- Circus-Folk
  http://circusfolk.freeservers.com

Civil Servants
Evidence of age was important to the Civil Service when making appointments and granting pensions. Its 60,000 'evidence of age' files are now held by the Society of Genealogists. A database is available at:
- Find My Past
  www.findmypast.com
  (click 'Specialist records' for details)

Clergy, Anglican
There have been numerous attempts to list clergy who served in particular parishes, deaneries, and dioceses. Local studies libraries and record offices frequently have manuscript lists for the parishes in their areas. Many lists have been

published in the proceedings of county historical and archaeological societies, and as record society volumes. Published lists can be identified in Stuart Raymond's series of county bibliographies. Currently, a major research project is compiling a database of all clergy between 1540 and 1835. In time, this database will be the authoritative listing of post-reformation clergy. See:

- CCEd: The Clergy of the Church of England Database
  www.theclergydatabase.org.uk

This project is described in:

- TOWEY, PETER. 'Researching Anglican clergymen: the clergy of the Church of England database', *Genealogists' magazine* **28**(7), 2005, p.310-12.

Since 1858, biographical information on all Church of England clergy has been regularly published in:

- *Crockford's clerical directory.* 1858- .

Runs of *Crockfords* are available in many libraries. A number of issues are now available as an 'Ancestry' database at **www.ancestry.co.uk**. Some issues are also available on CD.

The authoritative guide to other sources of information on Anglican clergy is:

- TOWEY, PETER. *My ancestor was an Anglican clergyman.* Society of Genealogists Enterprises, 2006.

See also:

- Biographical Sources for Anglican Clergy
  www.lambethpalacelibrary.org/files/Clergy_Guide.pdf

For the Diocese of London, consult:

- Sources for tracing Clergy and Lay People
  www.history.ac.uk/gh/clergy.htm

Clergy, Methodist

The central archives of the Methodist Church are now housed in the John Rylands Library of the University of Manchester. A great deal of information about Methodist ministers is available in this collection, which is the first place to check if you are researching an ancestor who was a Methodist clergyman. Its website includes an 'Index of Methodist Ministers', and the 'Methodist Archives Biographical Index'. Many connexional magazines in the collection include obituaries of clergymen. Visit:

- The University of Manchester: The John Rylands University Library: Methodist Collections
  www.library.manchester.ac.uk/specialcollections/collections/methodist

Clockmakers

There are many biographical dictionaries of clockmakers. These often relate to particular localities. See, for example,

- TYLER, E.J. *The clockmakers of Sussex*. Watch & Clock Book Society, [198-?].

At the national level, a dictionary of c.5,000 clockmakers is provided by:

- LOOMES, BRIAN. *The early clockmakers of Great Britain*. N.A.G. Press, 1981.

A fuller 'brief bibliography' is provided on the site of the:

- Worshipful Company of Clockmakers of London
  www.clockmakers.org/?page_id=85

The archives of this company are held by Guildhall Library. It also holds the library of the Antiquarian Horological Society, and a variety of other sources. See:

- Sources for Clock and Watchmakers at Guildhall Library
  www.cityoflondon.gov.uk/Corporation/LGNL_Services/ Leisure_and_culture/Libraries/City_of_London_libraries/ guildhall+library+guides.htm
  (click on 'Clock & Watchmakers')

Coalminers *see* Miners

Criminals

Criminals are well documented. The records of Assizes, Quarter Sessions, and the central courts are extensive. Most nineteenth century criminals are listed in TNA's series of criminal registers (HO27), which are based on returns from Clerks of the Peace, and run from 1805 to 1892. These have been indexed by Stuart Tamblin. Details are given at:

- HO 27: Criminal Registers
  www.fhindexes.co.uk/samples/criminal.pdf

An online database of these registers (also including registers in HO26) can be searched at:

- England and Wales Criminal Registers 1791-1892
  http://landing.ancestry.co.uk/intl/uk/criminal.aspx

Many thousand digitised images from the Old Bailey are available online:

- The Proceedings of the Old Bailey, 1674-1913
  www.oldbaileyonline.org

Another useful archive is calendared in:
- National Archives Local History Research Group. *Pardons and punish ments: judges reports on criminals, 1783 to 1831: HO (Home Office) 47.* 2 vols. List and Index Society **304-5**. 2004-5.

In the counties, jurisdiction was exercised by Quarter Sessions. Its records include sessions rolls, indictment books, calendars of prisoners, and a wide range of other sources. A select list of available Quarter sessions records is provided in:
- Gibson, Jeremy. *Quarter sessions records for family historians: a select list.* 5th ed. Family History Partnership, 2007.

A database of East Anglian prisoners can be found at:
- Victorian Crime and Punishment: Prisoner Records
  http://vcp.e2bn.org/prisoners

Many records were created by the police. For an example of what can be found, visit:
- City of Exeter Police Charge Book, Sep 1847 - 21 Feb 1849
  http://genuki.cs.ncl.ac.uk/DEV/Exeter/Police1/

The *Police gazette*, which commenced publication in 1772 as the *Public hue and cry*, has numerous reports of footpads, highwaymen, smugglers, house-breakers, murderers, forgers, larcenists, arsonists, rustlers, deserters and escaped convicts. A microfilm version is available in a number of libraries. It is published by:
- Adam Mathew Publications
  www.adam-matthew-publications.co.uk/news/documents/ PoliceGazette.pdf

The records of individual prisons may also prove useful. See, for example:
- Dartmoor Prison Records
  www.devon.gov.uk/index/councildemocracy/record_office/ record_offices_in_devon/guide_sources/crime/dartmoor_ prison.htm

In the late eighteenth and early nineteenth centuries, many convicts were transported to Australia. There are many relevant websites and databases. They can be found by visiting:
- Convicts to Australia: a Guide to Researching your Convict Ancestors
  www.convictcentral.com

Over 500,000 names taken from newspapers and journals are indexed in
- The Black Sheep Index
  www.blacksheepindex.co.uk

For detailed guides to criminal records, consult:

- WADE, STEPHEN. *Tracing your criminal ancestors: a guide for family historians.* Pen & Sword, 2009.
- HAWKINGS, DAVID. *Criminal ancestors: a guide to historical criminal records in England and Wales.* Alan Sutton, 1992.

Dentists

The names of dentists are recorded in the *Dentists' register*, which commenced in 1879, and continues today. This publication is available in libraries, but the British Dental Association Museum will search it and a number of other sources for dentists in your family. Visit:

- Was Your Ancestor a Dentist?
  www.bda.org/museum/enquiries/was-ancestor-dentist.aspx

East India Men

Between the sixteenth and the twentieth centuries, many men went to seek their fortune in India. Those who set their sights on a career with the East India Company often prepared themselves by studying at the Company's Haileybury College. Its records are described in:

- FARRINGTON, ANTHONY. *The records of the East India College, Haileybury, & other institutions.* HMSO, 1976.

There are numerous published directories listing employees of the East India Company and its successor, the colonial government of India. Many of these are listed in Raymond's *Occupational sources* (see above, p.6). See also:

- McEVOY, MICHAEL. 'East India registers and directories, 1768-1860', *Genealogists' magazine* **27**(12), 2003, p.536-9.

An index to some covenants and bonds entered into between the Company and its employees between 1607 and 1780 is described in:

- BAILEY, PETER. 'Early East India bonds and covenants', *Genealogists' magazine* **27**(9), 2003, p.406-14.

The records of the East India Company, and its successor, the India Office, are described on the British Library's website:

- India Office Records and Private Papers
  www.bl.uk/reshelp/findhelpregion/asia/india/indiaoffice records/indiaofficehub.html

If you need help and advice in researching your East Indiamen ancestors, join the:

- Families in British India Society
  www.fibis.org

Engineers

The Amalgamated Society of Engineers was founded in 1851, and continued under that name until 1920. It is now a part of the Amalgamated Engineering Union. Most of its records are held by the Modern Records Centre (see above, p.22-3). Its quarterly branch returns, however, are held by the Society of Genealogists, who are indexing them. For details, see:

• SQUIRE, DAVID. 'The records of the Amalgamated Society of Engineers', *Genealogists' magazine* **28**(10), 2006, p.435-40.

Fishermen

See also Seamen (Merchant Navy)

Apprentices in the trawling industry are discussed in:

• WILCOX, MARTIN. 'Opportunity or exploitation? Apprenticeship in the British trawler fisheries 1850-1936', *Genealogists' magazine* **28**(4), 2004, p.135-49.

Registers of fishing apprentices can sometimes be found in local record offices. For example, the North East Lincolnshire Archives have a register for Grimsby from 1880 to 1937. For more information, see:

• WILSON, JOHN. 'Registers of the sea fishing apprentices of Grimsby, 1880-1937', *Family history news & digest* **15**(1), 2005, p.7-10.

A comprehensive review of sources for fishermen is provided by:

• WILCOX, MARTIN. *Fishing and fishermen: A guide for family historians.* Pen & Sword, 2009.

Framework Knitters

The framework knitting machine was invented in 1589, and was a phenomenal success. The Worshipful Company of Framework Knitters was granted a royal charter in 1663. In 1828, it was reckoned that there were 20,000 framework knitters in Leicestershire alone. In the census, they are referred to as 'FWKs'. Several hundred FWK's gave evidence which is reported in the report from the *Royal Commission on the Condition of the Frame-work Knitters.* (1845). This report is in the Parliamentary papers series (see above, p.29)

Furniture Trades

The careers of furniture makers between 1877 and 1936 can be traced in the 12 issues of

• *The Post Office directory of the cabinet furniture and upholstery trades and the trades connected therewith.* Kelly & Co, 1877-1936. Some issues of this directory are entitled *Kelly's directory of ...*

Biographical details of English furniture makers may be found in:

- BEARD, GEOFFREY, & GILBERT, CHRISTOPHER, eds. *Dictionary of English Furniture Makers 1600-1840*. Furniture History Society, 1986.

Gunmakers

Stan Cook has compiled an index of gunmakers, based primarily on the records of London's Worshipful Company of Gunmakers. It also includes information drawn from the census, the Inland Revenue apprenticeship records, trade directories, wills, *etc*. Full details are given in:

- COOK, STAN. 'Gunmaking index', *Family history news & digest* **14**(4), 2004, p.166-9.

For a useful guide to the records of London's Worshipful Company of Gunmakers, see:

- HOLLAENDER, A.E.J. 'The archives of the Worshipful Company of Gunmakers of the City of London', *Archives* **1**(8), 1952, p.8-19.

Gypsies

Gypsies are often referred to as travellers, braziers, horse dealers, tinkers, *etc*. They are notoriously difficult to trace. Part of the problem is that they frequently changed their names, or at least told the authorities responsible for recording their names that they had done so. For a discussion of this problem, see:

- LEE, TERENCE. 'Gipsy genealogy: a study of name changing and other anomalies', *Genealogists' magazine* **26**(6), 1999, p.219-23.

Despite the difficulties, gypsies can be traced. Gypsy researchers should join the:

- Romany & Traveller Family History Society
  www.rtfhs.org.uk

A basic introduction to researching gypsy ancestors is provided by.

- FLOATE, SHARON SILLERS. *My ancestors were gypsies*. 2nd ed. Society of Genealogists, 2005.

It may also be worth searching the collections of the:

- Gypsy Lore Society
  http://sca.lib.liv.ac.uk/collections/colldescs/gypsy/index.htm

Horse Owners & Breeders

As far as I am aware, there is no specific word for a person who traces the genealogy of horses. However, the Shire Horse Society has been doing just that for over a cen-

tury. Its *Stud book* has been regularly published since 1880, and is available in major libraries. It gives not only the pedigrees of horses, but also the names and addresses of owners, breeders, and society members. See:
- SHORROCKS, JOHN. 'Stud books (for horses)', *Genealogists' magazine* **26**(12), 2000, p.519-10.

Landowners
Landowners are amongst the easiest people to trace, since they needed to be able to prove their title to land. Title deeds survive in profusion in most record offices. For a detailed guide, see:
- ALCOCK, N.W. *Old title deeds: a guide for local and family historians.* 2nd ed. Phillimore, 2001.

A wide variety of other sources for tracing landowners are available. The government organized a number of surveys of landownership in the nineteenth and twentieth centuries. The survey carried out in 1872/3 is reported in full in the *Parliamentary papers* series (see above, p.29). It lists everyone who owned an acre or more of land. Many portions of the return have been published in recent years, in both hard copy, on CD, and on the internet. The survey listed everyone who owned more than one acre of land, county by county. London was excluded. See:
- *Owners of land 1872/3 (England and Wales).* 2 vols. House of Commons Parliamentary papers 1874, **72**, pts 1 & 2. (C1097). HMSO, 1874.

This return is currently being transcribed for an online database:
- Return of Owners of Land in England and Wales
  http://uk-genealogy.org.uk/OwnersofLand.html

Other surveys included the tithe surveys of the 1830s and 1840s, the Valuation Office survey of 1910 to 1915, and the National Farm Survey of 1941-3. Records of the first two can be found in both TNA, and in county record offices. Records of the National Farm Survey are in TNA. A detailed guide to the records of all three surveys is provided by:
- BEECH, GERALDINE, & MITCHELL, ROSE. *Maps for family and local history: the records of the tithe, Valuation Office, and national farm surveys of England and Wales, 1836-1943.* 2nd ed. TNA, 2004.

Law Students
Law was a subject of interest to every gentleman in England between 1500 and 1900. The protection of their estates demanded at least a rudimentary knowledge of law, as did service as a Justice of the Peace or in other local offices. Many gentlemen spent some time at the Inns of Court in order to acquire the requisite

knowledge. Some, of course, went on to become lawyers, but many others returned to their estates to pursue the life of a country gentleman.

The admission registers of a number of Inns of Court have been printed, and are readily available in libraries. They include:

- FOSTER, JOSEPH. *The register of admissions to Gray's Inn, 1521-1889, together with the register of marriages in Gray's Inn Chapel 1695-1754.* Hansard Publishing Union, 1889.
- BAILDON, WILLIAM. *Records of the Honourable Society of Lincoln's Inn: Admissions 1420-1893, and chapel registers.* 2 vols. Lincoln's Inn, 1896.
- STURGESS, H.A.C. *Register of admissions to the Honourable Society of the Middle Temple, from the fifteenth century to the year 1944.* Butterworth, for the Society, 1949.

Admissions to the Inner Temple, 1547-1850 are listed on the web at:
- The Inner Temple Admissions Database
  www.innertemple.org.uk/archive/itad/index.asp

Lawyers

Records relating to lawyers are extensive. They include the records of the courts in which they served, admission registers of the Inns of Court (some of which are listed above), the various published *Law lists*, biographical dictionaries, and a wide variety of other sources. They are described in detail by:

- BROOKS, BRIAN, & HERBER, MARK. *My ancestor was a lawyer.* Society of Genealogists Enterprises, 2006.

See also:
- HOLBORN, GUY. *Sources of biographical information on past lawyers.* British & Irish Association of Law Librarians, 1999.
- How to Trace a Past Solicitor
  www.lawsociety.org.uk/productsandservices/libraryservices/ legalresearchguides.law
  (click title)

Librarians

Family historians owe a great debt to librarians. They are responsible for making available to us the hundreds of thousands of books and journals which may contain vital information for tracing our pedigrees. If a member of your family was a professional librarian in the twentieth century, the likelihood is that he or she was a member of the Library Association. Members' careers can be traced in the annual volumes of:

- *The Library Association year book.* 1891-2001.

Manorial Tenants

Most of us have ancestors who were manorial tenants. Manorial records survive from the thirteenth century until 1925, and contain an enormous amount of information about tenants: their dates of tenancy, their rents, the amount of land they held, their heirs. A detailed guide to their location and contents is provided by:
- PARK, PETER B. *My ancestors were manorial tenants*. [Rev ed.] Society of Genealogists Enterprises, 2005.

Mechanical Engineers

In order to become a member of the Institution of Mechanical Engineers, a proposal form had to be submitted. These can be consulted in the Institution's archives from 1847 to 1950. For an online catalogue, visit:
- I Mech E Archive
  www.imeche.org/library/archive.htm

Medical Professions

See also Physicians *and* Nurses
Hospital staff can be traced through the personnel records of hospitals. A union catalogue of hospital records is provided by:
- The Hospital Records Database
  www.nationalarchives.gov.uk/hospitalrecords

Lists of appointments, obituaries, and death notices, have been published regularly in the *Lancet* (1823-), the *British medical journal* (1857-), and the *Medical directory* (1845-1914). These journals are available in many reference libraries.

In the eighteenth century and earlier, medics required a licence to practise from a bishop. Many licences are indexed at:
- Lambeth Palace Library Research Guide: Medical Licences issued by the Archbishop of Canterbury 1535-1775
  www.lambethpalacelibrary.org/files/Medical_Licences.pdf

The extensive records for tracing medical personnel are fully described in:
- BOURNE, SUSAN, & CHICKEN, ANDREW H. *Records of the medical professions: a practical guide for the family historian*. The authors, 1994.

For doctors, reference may also be made to Alex Glendinning's website:
- Was your Ancestor a Doctor?
  user.itl.net/~glen/doctors.html

Members of Parliament

Members of Parliament are amongst the most extensively documented of all our ancestors. Many counties and cities have biographical dictionaries of their members. These can be identified in the county volumes of Stuart Raymond's county bibliographies. The authoritative biographical dictionaries, however, are those published by the History of Parliament Trust. These are widely available in libraries. Full details are given on the Trust's website:

- History of Parliament
  www.histparl.ac.uk

Millers
A 'millers and millwrights database', containing 30,000 entries, can be found on the family history page of:

- The Mills Archive
  www.millarchive.org/9family/portal.aspx

Miners
See also Bevin Boys

In the late nineteenth and early twentieth centuries, safety in mines was regularly inspected by Mines Inspectors. The appendices of their reports list the names of miners who died in mining disasters. These reports are included in the Parliamentary papers series, which have already been mentioned. Ian Winstanley has extracted 120,000 names from these reports, 1850-1972, for his 'National database of mining deaths in Great Britain' which can be found at:

- Coal Mining History Resource Centre
  www.cmhrc.co.uk

Similar lists for the counties of Cumberland, Westmorland, Northumberland, Durham, and the north of Yorkshire, are recorded by:

- Durham Mining Museum
  www.dmm.org.uk/mindex.htm

For a detailed guide to sources for coalminers, see:

- TONKS, DAVID. *My ancestor was a coalminer*. Society of Genealogists Enterprises, 2003.

Missionaries
There are over 400 collections of missionary archives in the UK. For details, see:

- Mundus: Gateway to Missionary Collections in the UK
  www.mundus.ac.uk

Many useful links can also be found at:

- Sources for Missionary and Church Archives
  www.soas.ac.uk/library/subjects/archives/links/missionary

Many Anglican missionaries served with the Church Missionary Society (now the Church Mission Society), and can be traced in its publications and archives. Its *CMS Proceedings* (1801-1921), which became *CMS Report* (1922-1961), and its *CMS Year Book* (1962-1980) which became *CMS Directory* (1981-) provided regular lists of missionaries and their stations. These publications, plus much else, are held in:

- CMS Archives
  www.cms-uk.org/Resources/CrowtherCentre/Archives/tabid/ 194/Default.aspx

Musicians
A wide range of resources are available for tracing musicians. For a basic introduction, consult:
- O'KANE, MARY. 'Musicians: orchestras, organists and oratorios', *Your family tree* **45**, 2006, p.54-7.

Nurses
See also Medical Professions *and* Prisoners of War
The state registration of nurses commenced under the Nurses Act, 1919. This established the General Nursing Council, which opened its *Register of Nurses* on 30 September 1921. Nurses who were then working were allowed to register until the end of 1923. Thereafter, nurses had to pass an examination in order to be registered. Entries in the register give the nurse's name, registered number, permanent address, qualifications, and the date and place of registration. It is available in many reference libraries. TNA holds copies of the register prior to 30th November 1973. For more information, see:
- Civilian Nurses and Nursing Services
  www.nationalarchives.gov.uk/catalogue/researchguidesindex.asp
  (click title)

For an overall view of the history of nursing, visit:
- Nursing and Midwifery History UK
  http://web.archive.org/web/20080108103651rn_1/ www.shef.ac.uk/~nmhuk/

The most important archive for the nursing profession is held by the Royal College of Nursing. Its website includes a database of historic nursing journals. Click 'online databases' at:
- RCN Archives
  www.rcn.org.uk/development/rcn_archives

London Metropolitan Archives also holds a wide range of nursing records. They are described in:

- HOWLETT, BRIDGET. 'Records of nurses and nursing: resources in London Metropolitan Archives, 1556-1939', *Genealogists' magazine* **26**(6), 1999, p.213-6.

Patients

Hospitals have preserved many records of patients. These are frequently closed to inquiries for 50 or 100 years. In some cases, however, they survive from the eighteenth century, and can provide most interesting information to the family historian. Many can be located on:

- The Hospital Records Database
  www.nationalarchives.gov.uk/hospitalrecords/

For the London Hospital, see:

- Patient Records of the London Hospital
  www.aim25.ac.uk/cgi-bin/search2?coll_id=3908&inst_id=23

Pedlars

Pedlars were men and women who travelled from town to town, and from house to house, selling goods. Under the Pedlars Act 1871, they required a certificate licensing them to trade. These certificates had to be endorsed by the police in the places they visited. Registers of pedlars' endorsements survive in local archives. These give names of pedlars, their addresses (often just the parish), the police district which issued the certificate, and the dates of issue and expiry. A register from Exeter has been published:

- *Register of pedlars' endorsements 1871-1875.* Devon Family History Society, 2006.

Pewterers

Pewter is an amalgam of tin, copper, and antimony. Between the sixteenth and the nineteenth centuries, it was commonly used for tableware. Pewterers often made their mark on the wares they produced. These marks are useful sources of information for family historians. Many are listed in:

- COTTERELL, HOWARD HERSCHEL. *Old pewter: its makers and marks in England, Scotland and Ireland. An account of the old pewterer and his craft.* B.T.Batsford, 1929. Reprinted 1968.

Pharmacists

The *Pharmaceutical journal* has regularly published lists of the members and associates of the Pharmaceutical Society of Great Britain. An outline of the history of the profession, with some hints for genealogists, is given in:

- Tracing People and Premises in Pharmacy
  www.rpsgb.org/pdfs/tracing.pdf

Photographers

The Museum of London's PhotoLondon database has biographical notes on about 9,000 photographers of the nineteenth century, presumably based on its own collections:

- PhotoLondon: The Database of 19th Century Photographers and Allied Trades in London, 1841-1901
  www.photolondon.org.uk

Physicians

See also Medical Professions

The annals of the College of Physicians include details of 714 physicians whom the College accused of practising illegally in London. Their names have been extracted to create a biographical database:

- Physicians and Irregular Medical Practitioners in London 1550-1640
  www.british-history.ac.uk/source.aspx?pubid=107

Pipemakers

When Raleigh introduced tobacco to the English, he did not realise that he was creating a new occupation - that of pipemaker. Nor did he realise that archaeologists would specialise in studying the remnants of pipemakers' work. Their studies sometimes result in lists of pipemakers, which could be of help to family historians. For example, a 48 page listing of pipemakers is included in:

- OSWALD, ADRIAN. 'The archaeology and economic history of English clay tobacco pipes', *Journal of the British Archaeological Association* 3rd series **22**, 1959, p.40-102.

For pipemakers whose pipes have been found in London excavations, see:
- Clay Tobacco Pipe Makers Marks from London
  www.museumoflondon.org.uk/claypipes/index.asp

Policemen

Generally speaking, the survival of police records is sporadic. If you are fortunate, you may be able to find discipline books, attestation papers, pension records, and other personal files. Some information may also be found in occurrence books, general order books, Chief Constables' annual reports, and a variety of other sources. A comprehensive listing of surviving records is provided by:

- SHEARMAN, ANTONY. *My ancestor was a policeman.* Society of Genealogists, 2000.

See also:
- *Guide to the archives of the police forces of England and Wales* / Ian Bridgeman & Clive Emsley
  www.open.ac.uk/Arts/history/policing/police-archives-guide/index.html
- O'NEILL, JOSEPH. 'The police', *Family history monthly* **80**, 2002, p.36-40.

Police archives are often found in county record offices. There are, however, an increasing number of police force museums. These usually have web pages, and may hold relevant information. For example, many photographs of Kent policemen can be found at:.
- Kent Police Museum Photo Archive
  www.kent-police-museum.co.uk/gallery/albums.php

A database with 500,000 unique entries relating to the London Metropolitan Police can be found at:
- Police Orders
  www.policeorders.co.uk

A number of useful websites are linked at:
- The Police History Society
  www.policehistorysociety.co.uk

Postmen

The 'British Postal Museum and Archive' **www.postalheritage.org.uk** has already been mentioned. It holds extensive personnel records relating to Post Office employees. Amongst much else, these include extensive records of pensions, especially for the period since 1859. Also important are its appointment books and establishment books. These sources provide valuable information about a postman's career, such as years and place(s) of service, wages, appointments held, conduct, and date of birth. The website also has a war memorials database. For a detailed discussion of the Museum's archives, see:
- SQUELCH, KEVIN. 'The archives of the British Post Office', *Family history news & digest* **10**(3), 1996, p.126-8.

Prisoners of War

TNA holds a variety of records relating to prisoners of war. These are discussed in two 'research guides':
- Prisoners of War, British, 1939-1953
- Prisoners of War, British, c1760-1919

These may be found at **www.nationalarchives.gov.uk/catalogue/ researchguidesindex.asp** (click titles).

Records of prisoners of war were also kept by the Red Cross, which was established after Henri Dunant, a young Swiss businessman, witnessed appalling suffering on the battlefield of Solferino in 1859. Its humanitarian work has created records relating to both prisoners of war, and nurses.

The Red Cross gathers information on prisoners of war so that family members can be put in touch, and to ensure that accurate information about their captivity is held. There are over 7,000,000 cards relating to First World War prisoners alone. These are held by the:

- International Committee of the Red Cross
  www.icrc.org

During the First World War, the Red Cross also administered many hospitals, which were staffed by Voluntary Aid Detachment (VAD) nurses. Women VADs took on roles such as ambulance drivers, cooks, and telephonists, as well as the more conventional nursing duties. Index cards for VAD nurses, giving dates and places of service, and the nature of the work carried out, are now held by the:

- British Red Cross
  www.redcross.org.uk/standard.asp?id=3423.

The history of the Red Cross, and details of the surviving records for both nurses and prisoners of war, are given in:

- PUGH, HELEN. 'International Red Cross and Red Crescent movement', *Family history news & digest* **13**(1), 2001, p.12-14.

Railwaymen

In the late nineteenth century, railways opened people's horizons, making it easy to travel long distances in search of work. They also provided employment for many thousand people who otherwise might have experienced difficulty in finding regular employment. A variety of sources are available which can be used to trace them. A detailed discussion is provided in

- HARDY, FRANK. *My ancestor was a railway worker*. Society of Genealogists Enterprises, 2009.

The personnel records of railwaymen survive in great profusion. They are listed in:

- RICHARDS, TOM. *Was your grandfather a railwayman?* 4th ed. F.F.H.S., 2002. New edition forthcoming, to be published by the Family History Partnership.

See also:

- HAWKINGS, DAVID T. *Railway ancestors: a guide to the staff records of the railway companies of England and Wales*. 2nd ed. History Press, 2008.

- Tracking Railways Archive Project
  www.trap.org.uk/index.html

The experts in this field of research are the Railway Ancestors Family History Society. If your ancestors were railwaymen, you should join them!
- Railway Ancestors Family History Society
  www.railwayancestors.org.uk

Refugees
Refugees are not just a modern phenomenon. The word was actually coined several hundred years ago, when the Huguenots were fleeing persecution in France. Many of them were relieved through the Threadneedle Street Church, whose register is printed in:
- HANDS, A.P., & SCOULOUDI, IRENE, eds. *French protestant refugees relieved through the Threadneedle Street Church, London, 1681-1687.* Publications of the Huguenot Society of London **49**. 1971.

Royal Marines
Royal Marines are soldiers who serve at sea. Many records relating to them are held at TNA, whose website **www.nationalarchives.gov.uk/catalogue/researchguidesindex.asp** has a number of research guides, including:
- Royal Marines: How to Find a Division
- Royal Marines: Officers' Service Records
- Royal Marines: Other Ranks' Service Records
- Royal Marines: Further Areas of Research

For a detailed guide, including information about records held by other repositories, see:
- DIVALL, KEN. *My ancestor was a Royal Marine.* Society of Genealogists Enterprises, 2008.

Seamen (Merchant Navy) *See also* Fishermen
The main source for tracing details of merchant seamen, especially from the eighteenth century, are the archives of the Registry of Shipping and Seamen. These archives include service registers, 1835-1972, apprenticeship records, medals, and crew lists. TNA holds many of these archives. There are a number of research guides on its webpage **www.nationalarchives.gov.uk/catalogue/research guidesindex.asp**. These include:
- Merchant Seamen: Records of the RGSS, A Guide to Research Guides
- Merchant Seamen: Abbreviations Found in the RGSS Registers
- Merchant Seamen: Interpreting the Voyages in the Registers of Seamen's Tickets and the Alphabetical Registers of Masters

- Merchant Seamen: Interpreting Voyage Details in the Registers of Officer's Services
- Merchant Seamen: Interpreting Voyage Details in the Registers of Seamen, Series II
- Merchant Seamen: Log books, Agreements and Crew Lists after 1861
- Merchant Seamen: Medals and Honours
- Merchant Seamen: Officers Service Records, 1845-1965
- Merchant Seamen: Registers of Service, 1835-1857
- Merchant Seamen: Sea Service Records, 1913-1972
- Merchant Shipping: Crew Lists and Agreements, 1747-1860

Crew lists and agreements record the names of crews serving on particular ships for a particular period or voyage. In the nineteenth century, these lists had to be sent to the Board of Trade. They have survived, but there are so many that they have had to be dispersed to about 50 different repositories. An introduction to these lists is provided by:

- Crew List Index Project
  www.crewlist.org.uk

A database on the Somerset Archives & Record Office site lists 35,000 names:
- Bridgwater Shipping Crew Lists
  www1.somerset.gov.uk/archives/
  (click 'online catalogue & indexes')

Distressed mariners could obtain relief by petitioning Trinity House. Those who did so are listed in:
- *Trinity House petitions: a calendar of the records of the Corporation of Trinity House, London, in the library of the Society of Genealogists.* Society of Genealogists, 1987.

Other Trinity House records relating to pensioners, pilotage, lighthouse keepers, *etc.*, are available. Details are given at:
- Trinity House: Genealogy
  www.trinityhouse.co.uk/corporation/genealogy.html

A variety of records are held by the National Maritime Museum. These include, for example, registers of engineers' certificates of passing and renewals 1905–1930, records of the Merchant Navy Reserve Pool for World War II, and Marine Society registers of apprentices, eighteenth-twentieth centuries. For details, see:
- Merchant Navy
  www.nmm.ac.uk/server/show/conWebDoc.588

The Merseyside Maritime Museum also holds relevant archives, and has a number of useful leaflets on its site. These include, for example, 'Records of training ships and educational establishments', 'Researching seafaring ancestors in World War One', and 'Privateering'. Visit:

- Merseyside Maritime Museum: Maritime Archives and Library: List of Information Sheets
  www.liverpoolmuseums.org.uk/maritime/archive/listGuides.aspx

For the twentieth century, about 1,250,000 mariners, 1918-41, are recorded on:

- The Central Index Register of Merchant Seamen
  www.southampton.gov.uk/s-leisure/artsheritage/history/ archives/collections/merhantseamen/centralindex.aspx

There are numerous other sources for tracing seafarers. The authoritative guide to them is provided by:

- WATTS, CHRISTOPHER, & WATTS, MICHAEL J. *My ancestor was a merchant seaman*. 2nd ed. Society of Genealogists, 2002.

Reference may also be made to:

- HOGG, PETER L. *Using merchant ship records for family historians*. Basic facts about ... series. F.F.H.S., 1997.
- *Tracing your family history: Merchant Navy*. Imperial War Museum, 2000.

Seamen (Royal Navy)

Records of men who served in the Royal Navy survive from the seventeenth century in TNA. For officers, there are service records, certificates of service, passing certificates, applications for appointment, records of promotion, pay registers, and a wide variety of other sources. Sources for ratings are fewer, but service records are available from 1802. Some sources relate to both officers and men. There are, for example, records of medals issued, casualties, and pensions. Archives relating to Greenwich Hospital and Chatham Chest have much to tell us. The wills of 35,000 Royal Naval seamen have been digitised for TNA's 'Documents Online' page **www.nationalarchives.gov.uk/documentsonline**.

There are many useful guides to sources on TNA's website **www.national archives.gov.uk/catalogue/researchguidesindex.asp**. Amongst others, you should read:

- Royal Navy: Commissioned Officers' Pay and Pension Records
- Royal Navy: Officers' Service Records
- Royal Navy: Officers' Service records, First World War, 1914-1918, and Confidential Reports, 1893-1943

- Royal Navy: Ratings Service Records, 1667-1923
- Royal Navy: Ratings' Pension Records
- Royal Navy: Warrant Officers' Pension Records

Another important source is the published *Navy list,* which began its career in 1782 as *Steel's navy list,* and still continues publication today. Copies are held in many libraries, as well as in TNA. Libraries also hold numerous biographical dictionaries (see above, p.26). If you want to check whether your ancestor was a naval lieutenant before 1902, consult:
- PAPPALARDO, BRUNO. *Royal Navy lieutenants' passing certificates 1691-1902.* 2 pts. List & Index Society **289**. 2001.

If your ancestors were naval men, you should begin your search by reading:
- PAPPALARDO, BRUNO. *Tracing your naval ancestors.* Readers guide **24**. Public Record Office, 2003.

See also:
- *Tracing your family history: Royal Navy.* Imperial War Museum, 1999.

For a wider perspective on naval records, it may be worth studying:
- COCK, RANDOLPH, & RODGER, N.A.M., eds. *A guide to the naval records of the UK.* Institute of Historical Research / T.N.A., 2006.

Servants
In the nineteenth century, domestic service was a major occupation. Perhaps a third of all women spent some time in service. There are many sources which can be used to trace them. These are fully described in:
- HORN, PAMELA. *My ancestor was in service.* Society of Genealogists Enterprises, 2009.

Many nineteenth-century servants were recruited from the London Foundling Hospital. Records relating to them are descibed in:
- HORN, PAMELA. `Victorian servants' lives & mothers' petitions to the London Foundling Hospital', *Genealogists magazine* **29**(8), 2008, p.293-7.

After the First World War, it was difficult to recruit domestic servants. The government's response was to establish a number of servant training centres, which fitted trainees to work as maids. Some records of these centres survive in TNA, class LAB2. They list course participants, giving names, addresses, and details of former employment. Sometimes they indicate where trainees found subsequent employment, and they may give other personal details. For a full discussion, see:

- HORN, PAMELA. 'Hunting the servants: the role of servant training centres between the wars', *Genealogists' magazine* **26**(8), 1999, p.296-300.

In the seventeenth and eighteenth centuries, many young people emigrated to North America. They often went as indentured servants. In return for passage and maintainance, they entered indentures which bound them to serve as servants for a specified term of years. 10,000 emigrants, mainly from the West Country, South Wales, and the West Midlands, are listed in:

- COLDHAM, PETER WILSON. *The Bristol registers of servants sent to foreign plantations 1654-1686.* Genealogical Publishing, 1988.

Many others can be found online at the:
- Immigrant Servants Database
  www.immigrantservants.com

Shareholders
The records of companies include registers of shareholders. An unusual related source is provided by the 'probate books' of the Great Western Railway. These record the evidence that was required to transfer shareholdings when ownership changed due to death, bankruptcy, marriage, or other reason. These registers are held by the Society of Genealogists, and are being indexed. See:

- HARDY, FRANK. 'Great Western Railway probate books: an introduction', *Genealogists' magazine* **27**(9), 2003, p.404-14.

Shoemakers
An 'index of shoemakers and shoemaking firms from the Roman period onwards' is held by Northampton Museum. Brief details are at:

- Northampton Borough Council: Museum Collections: The Shoe Collection
  www.northampton.gov.uk/site/scripts/documents_info.php?documentID=311&pageNumber=1

Soldiers, Discharged
Various acts of Parliament between 1749 and 1816 gave discharged soldiers the right to trade in towns and cities whose by-laws otherwise restricted that right to freemen. Such traders were known as King's freemen. They had to obtain a certificate of entitlement to trade by producing their discharge papers and other evidence. In London, these were retained, and records of about 4000 King's freemen are now held by the London Metropolitan Archives. See:

- ALDOUS, VIVIENNE. 'Records of King's freemen in the City of London, in the 18th and 19th centuries', *Genealogists' magazine* **27**(9), 2003, p.415-21.

- Kings Freemen and their Records in CLRO
  **www.cityoflondon.gov.uk/Corporation/LGNL_Services/
  Leisure_and_culture/Records_and_archives/Visitor_
  nformation/free_information_leaflets.htm**
  (click title)

Solicitors
See Lawyers

Sportsmen
Cricketers, footballers, and other sportsmen are relatively famous, and often well documented. There are many biographical dictionaries devoted to them. Histories of individual clubs abound. Sporting periodicals often list teams, giving the names of players. *Wisden's cricketers almanac*, for instance, has published many obituaries since 1892. These are available at
- Wisden
  www.cricinfo.com/almanack/almanack-splash.html

There is also a printed edition:
- GREEN, BENNY, ed. *The Wisden book of obituaries: obituaries from Wisden cricketers almanac 1892-1985*. Queen Anne Press, 1986.

Numerous other books on cricketers are listed in:
- PADWICK, E.W. *A bibliography of cricket*. 2nd ed. Library Association, 1984.

For footballers, see:
- My Ancestor was a Footballer
  **www.nationalfootballmuseum.com/pages/research/
  familyhistory.htm**

Stonemasons
The Friendly Society of Operative Stonemasons was formed in 1833. In the twentieth century, it merged with various other trade unions, and is now the Union of Construction Allied Trades and Technicians. Its records are deposited in two repositories. The Working Class Movement Library **www.wcml.org.uk** has its annual audits from 1865 to 1918. These include details of new members, deceased members, accidents, and superannuated members. Admission registers 1886-1911 are held by the Modern Records Centre **www2.warwick.ac.uk/services /library/mrc/subject_guides/family_history/stone**.

For a brief review of sources for stonemasons, consult:
* LISLE, NICOLA. 'Monumental tasks', *Family history monthly* **148**, 2007, p.38-40.

Teachers
Teachers can frequently be traced in the records of the institutions which trained them. The National Society for Promoting the Education of the Poor in the Principles of the Church of England, together with the nonconformist British and Foreign School Society, were important voluntary organizations which trained teachers and established elementary schools before the state took over reponsibility for education. The National Society's archives are held by the Church of England Record Centre in Bermondsey, and includes an index of teachers trained by the Society, 1812-1855. For details, visit:
* National Society for Promoting Religious Education: Archives
www.natsoc.org.uk/society/archives.html

The British and Foreign School Society's annual report for 1877 includes a list of all its trainees since 1810. Its journal, the *Educational record*, reported the names of students who passed its teacher certificate examinations; it also reported appointments in its schools. Various other records survive in its archives. See:
* BARTLE, GEORGE F. 'The records of the British and Foreign School Society', *Genealogists' magazine* **23**(3), 1989, p.102-3.

There is an online catalogue of the Society's archives at:
* British & Foreign School Society
www.bfss.org.uk

Teachers who worked in private schools were frequently trained by the College of Preceptors. For details of its archive, visit:
* Helpers: College of Preceptors
http://helpers.shl.lon.ac.uk/description04.php

Many teachers in private schools joined the Association of Assistant Masters. Its archive has been indexed, and is described by:
* Helpers: Association of Assistant Masters
http://helpers.shl.lon.ac.uk/description07.php

Theatrical Workers
See also Circus Workers
Tracing ancestors who worked in the theatre is not easy. There are many biographical dictionaries for performers (see above, p.26). Playbills and biographical notices in newspapers provide important sources of information. Journals such as

the *Era* (1838-1939) and the *Stage* (1881-1959) carried many obituaries. Consult:

- NEWMAN, PAUL. 'The *Era* newspaper as a source of entertainment history', *Genealogists' magazine* **26**(12), 2000, 488-9.
- The Stage Archive
  https://archive.thestage.co.uk

There are a number of large collections of playbills, posters, programmes and other ephemera which can be used to trace performers. Some are listed above under Circus Workers. See also:

- British Library Literary and Theatrical Collections
  www.bl.uk/reshelp/findhelprestype/manuscripts/ mssliterarytheatre/msslittheatre.html
- The Mander and Mitchenson Theatre Collection
  www.mander-and-mitchenson.co.uk

A detailed guide to theatrical sources is provided by:

- RUSTON, ALAN. *My ancestor worked in the theatre*. Society of Genealogists Enterprises, 2005.

Tradesmen

The *London gazette* carried many official notices relating to tradesmen. For example, those who held warrants of appointment from the crown were regularly listed. Notices concerning the dissolution of partnerships were posted. All bankruptcies were gazetted. The *Gazette* can be searched at:

- Gazettes
  www.gazettes-online.co.uk

There are a variety of other records for tradesmen who went bankrupt. These are outlined in two research guides, 'Bankruptcy Records After 1869', and 'Bankrupts and Insolvent Debtors, 1710-1869', on TNA's site
  www.nationalarchives.gov.uk/catalogue/researchguidesindex.asp
  (click titles).

Volunteer Soldiers

In 1794, patriotic fervour was at its height as a French invasion appeared to be imminent. Many people volunteered to serve in the army on a part-time basis, whilst continuing their civilian occupation. Many registers of volunteers survive, not only in TNA, but also in county record offices, military museums, and elsewhere. The register of the Dorset Volunteers is held by the Military Museum in Dorchester. It lists each volunteer's name, abode, occupation, date of enrolment, and unit. It has been fully transcribed and indexed. See:

- *The Volunteer soldiers, Dorset, 1794 to 1798*. Somerset & Dorset Family History Society, 1994.

Watermen

If you wanted to work in a boat on the River Thames, you had to be a member of the London Company of Watermen and Lightermen. The Company was established by act of Parliament. Its archives are in Guildhall Library. Members can be traced through the Company's 'apprenticeship binding' indexes. Registers of lighters, passenger boats, and barges, record the names of owners. There are also pension records and a variety of other sources. Full details are given in:

- LEGON, JAMES W. *My ancestors were Thames watermen: a guide to tracing your Thames watermen and lightermen ancestors*. 2nd ed. Society of Genealogists Enterprises, 2008.

See also:

- Records of the Company of Watermen and Lightermen at Guildhall Library **www.history.ac.uk/gh/water.htm**

Index